I dedicate this book to those who stuck by me.

You know who you are. Thank you. A million times, thank you.

Foreword

Hi dear reader, thanks for picking up this little book of poetry.

During my lifetime I've been very lucky in some ways, and in some ways, not. What I hope to share with you as you go through this book is an honest account of my writings during a time of realisation and recovery.

Through therapy, relationship fallouts, and family difficulties, poetry gave me a place to vent, to relay and to express my feelings through written words.

I hope to inspire you in some way, that whatever it is you go through, whatever life throws at you, you have the power in yourself to overcome it.

But firstly allow the pain to walk through the chapters of necessary processing, before you find your true self again.

Tomorrow

Tomorrow isn't now
Pain is temporary, somehow
Don't hesitate to forget,
That your true self is not yet met

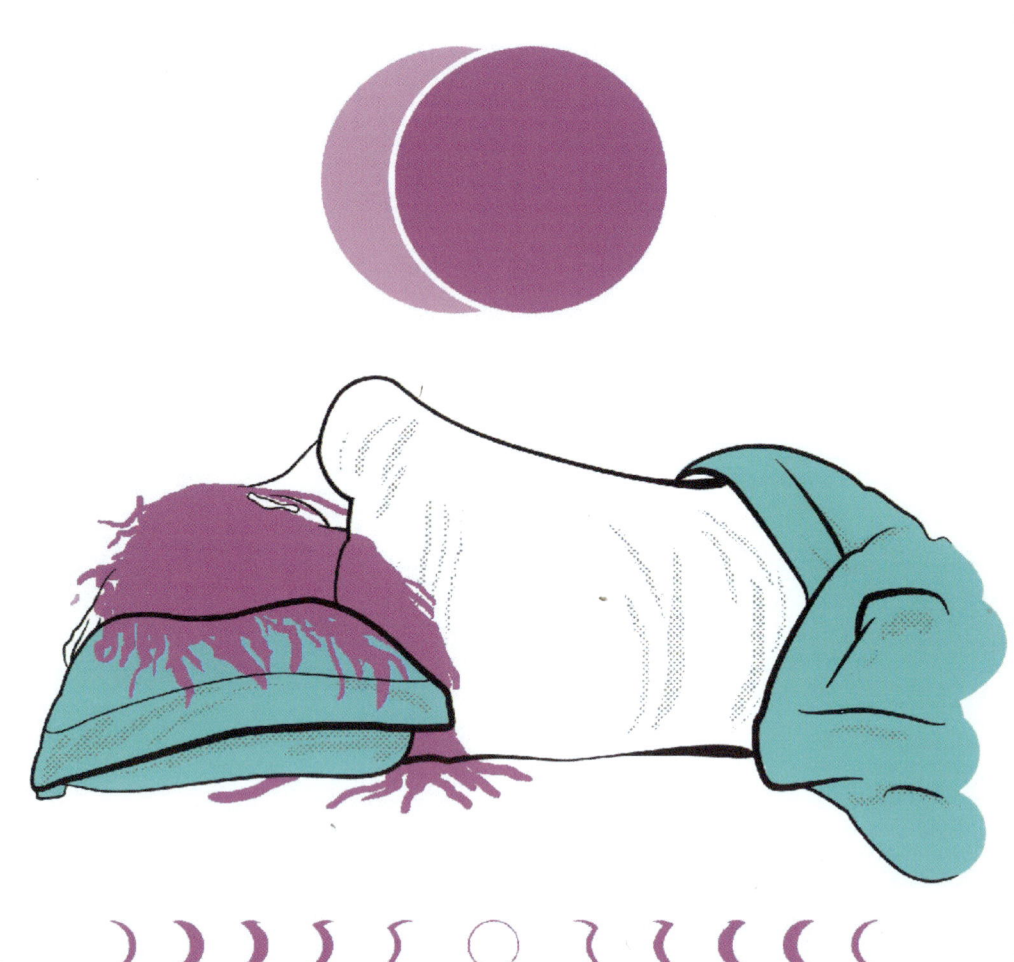

The Crossover

I never meant for it to crossover
Only to lie in bed and just turnover

The nights are never meant to match the days
The evenings aren't sent to marry tomorrow's dismay

Downward spiral and big bruises
The tears and tantrums where everyone loses

Such pain is held for release to endure
Her strong demise is no longer demure

Nothing to see here, she says in dismissal
Masking the pain of powerful contrition

What's night must be day, for then I can see
But for this evening I pray that my trauma lets me be

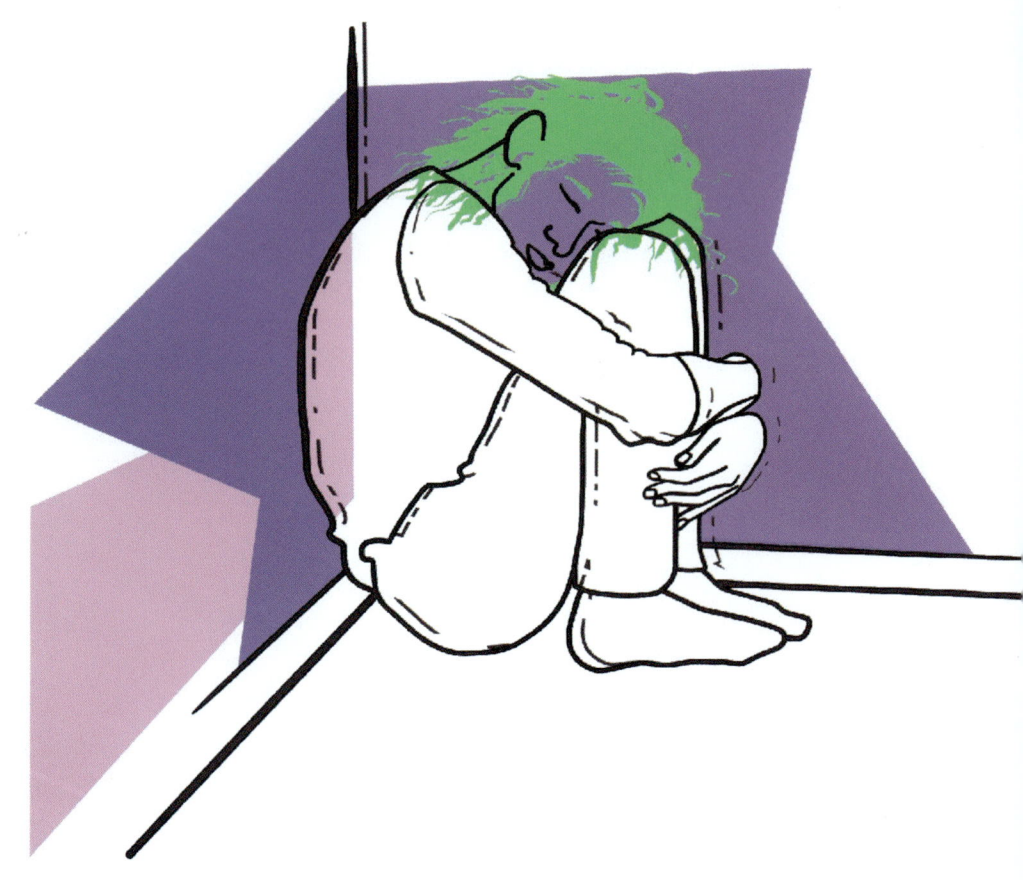

Dear young girl

Dear young girl
Who hurt you
Who hurt you

Dear young girl
I hear you
I hear you

Dear young girl
Such pain
Such pain

Dear young girl
The shame
The shame

Figure

What did the figure represent
That caused her such discontent
What trauma did the figure show to her soul
What did the figure do to her goal

Figure you are dark, I hate you so
Yet I'm afraid to tell you, I'm afraid to know
Two bodies in one, assault and abuse
Oh, figure what can we do to form a truce?

You may not be there, but I see feel and hear
You are to me figure, what I want to disappear
You are harsh words, you are emotion
You are psychical pain, family commotion

Will you be there forever? Like an old oak tree?
You are a concrete shadow
My figure and me

Age Five

If I could tell you
What strength you have
That your mind is an intelligent
And glorious map

Of inspiration and spirit,
Of confidence and poise
I know you're in pain
And cannot shut out the noise

But you are as strong as an Ox,
And will continue to be
My inner child
You're everything to me

There it is

So there it is
The official diagnosis
Years of stress
Without a single prognosis

There it is
So I lay here in shock
Processing the truth
Whilst memories they flock

So there it is
It was there all along
The ins and the outs
Another day of being strong

So there it is
It all makes sense now
The slots into place
I just knew, somehow

So there it is
But not an absolute
So treatment begins
Confusions' commute

So there it is
It's now it's then
I'm aiming for a future
For now, take ten

So there it is
So we begin
You've come this far
But tonight, stay in

Forgiveness

Does pain still show?
Yes, it may not go
Does it still make you feel that way?
Yes, every night and by the light of day

What can I do?
Think about you
So forget? Let it be?
No, forgiveness, be free

What's done is done So we don't care?
Not that, but your heart is to share
Holding on, for principles sake
Whom for, I ask? What is at stake?

Open the cage, let that bird fly
Black crow I see, no longer be shy
Drop the pain and your shoulders, do you see?
It's lightweight, it's forgiveness
Dear soul, be free

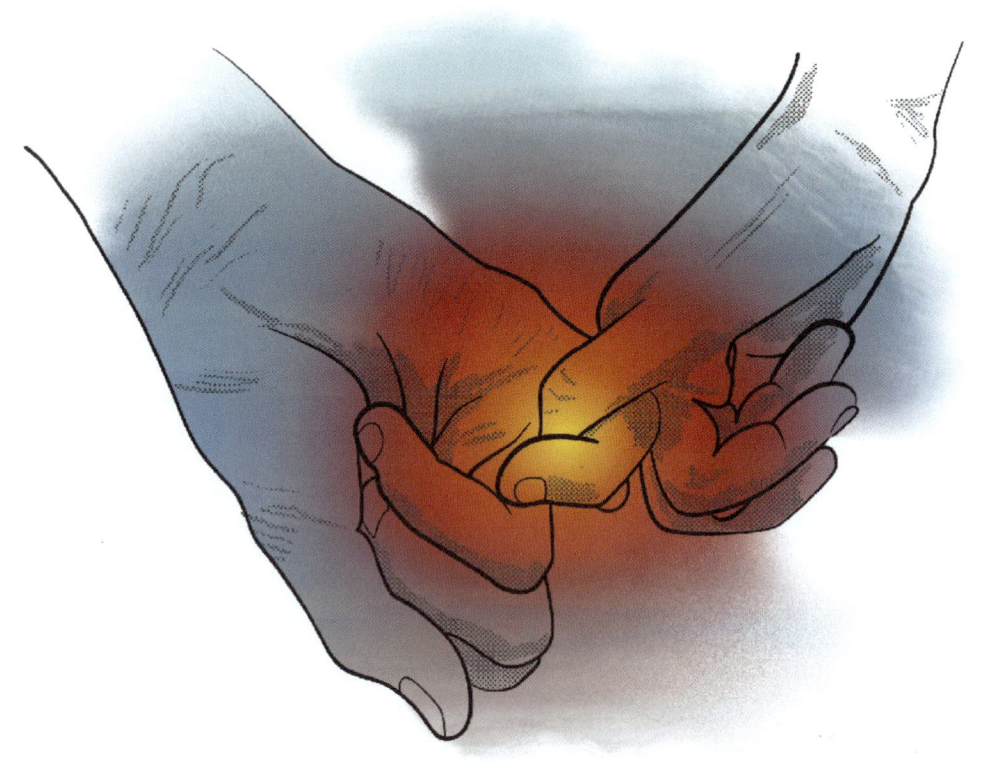

But why?

But why should one be hasty

To ignore those feelings

If it is you I want I shall fight

To haunt the doubts

Which would let you go

Tired

Tiredness plus one
Not an element of fun
Not just the lack of sleep
But a mental demon creeps

Why does it lay there
Not here but forever shared
The silence is dull and grey
No fear of a rainy day

For rain in comparison
Holds the medicine
Nature is but great
It's the demon that
Makes me late

Tiredness & the addition
Is a mental expedition
Not one but two
throws both barrels at you

Is it a case of both?
Do I take a life long oath?
Surely not, please
I need some path of ease

Let me find peace
For now, at least
Morning shall come
Hopeful joy, for some

Now

She now knew what

She could be

The doubt and fear

Were long gone,

From he

It's happening

It's happening, it's good
It's doing what it should
She knows, now
what she never did somehow

It's happening, the pause
No search for empathy cause
Because there shalt not
be one blessing from he

I know it's tough
this happening is rough
But you know, you do
That you can now see
Right through

The plate is yours
The happening it pours
Heavy to bear
Behind a solemn stare
But you know
The happening
The truth it is out
It is only in your body
that there must not be doubt

He knows underneath
Hiding behind wretched wreath
That the cause of death
Is the lies through gritted teeth
I see it what it's for
The happening and more
I know me, I know you
and I know what to do

It is time It's here
This feels so sincere
You now know not to seek
What you know is bleak

The acceptance comes from you
Rid of all expectations
The happening is here
With its painful ramifications

Take the first step child
Take it for yourself
Do not lie there dying
On the desperate crying shelf

Well done! There it is
You've got it, let's go
We can now move on
To the path where we grow

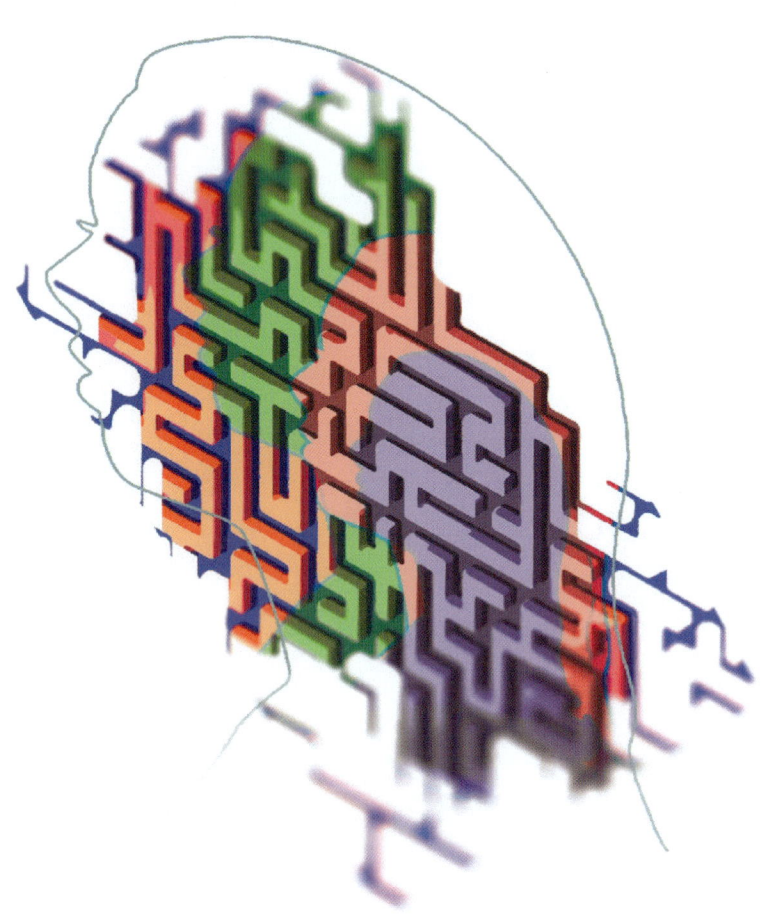

You'll never know

She did not know what she could be
Only doubt was what seemed to be
One day perhaps her mind would free
But for now remains only uncertainty

She did not know what she could be
What have you done right is all she'd see
That hurt that pain is not solved by immediate glee
Nor positive comments that came to she

Be proud

Be proud of what you've done my girl
Look how far you've come
The road is never straight my girl
But you're here, til kingdom come

Be nice to yourself sweet child
It's okay to have ups and the downs
Look at that resilience sweet child
How smiles have come out of frowns

What an incredibly strong lady
Look at her in all her strength
What they say isn't your truth strong lady
Your potential knows such length

I am the person I want to be
Say it with me, say it with me
Look in the mirror with awe inspiring glee
I am the person I want to be

Take it easy, no pressure my lovely
You've got unbelievable power
Look at how you keep moving forward my lovely
You're at the top of your mastery tower

Just words

I hate the word process
A pressure one must address
I don't want it to undress
My darkest thoughts nonetheless

The acceptance of ups and downs
Bring forth the heaviest of frowns
'You're coming on leaps and bounds'
They said, unbearable mixed sounds

Inconsistencies you don't see
Why do I hide from you, from me
The struggle of just being free
To relax, to breathe, to be

I read each and every emotion
Believe me, I dread the commotion
Do you not understand this notion?
There is no magic potion

How dare you bury my sadness
Accuse me of utter madness
All I needed was gladness
Not terror, horror, badness

Listen to what who has to say?
Who knows what it'll be like today
Only silence quiets the fray
Only silence will dilute the dismay

Don't kill me with words unspoken
Your eyes depict a vile token
That stirs leaving me heartbroken
You have no idea what you've awoken

Please allow me to heal but hear this
The process none can dismiss
Well accept that word, I shall not miss
The importance of avoiding the abyss

Now it's accepting what's to come
That some days will be dark, some glum
But that does not mean, my chum
That you will not one day, feel the sun

No longer

No longer can I lean on you
No longer I ask, what for?
Your love and lies create painful ties
It's time to close the door

No longer can I relate to you
No longer is that connection
No longer can I make sense of it all
I don't crave your love or affection

No longer do I mourn the loss
Of what could and should have been
No longer do I fight for my time
To be heard, listened to and seen

I love you and hold you forever
In a mind full of hurt and despair
But no longer can I carry this out
It's better, if you were no longer there

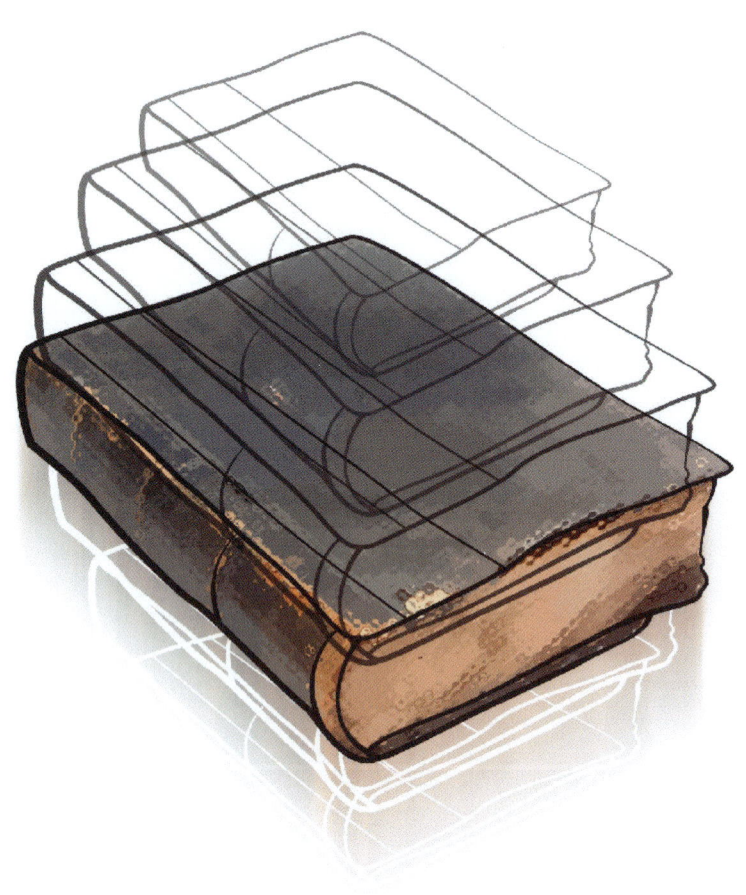

The Never End

Oh you're still sad?
You still weep?
You're still late from lack of sleep?
It's time to move on
Time to get going
Well then is my grief worth knowing?
Why doesn't my pain ring true?
Would it be different if it happened to you?

All I want is to hear, I'll still be there
Even if I'm not near
Not what you've done, not what you've said
This trauma I feel is far from dead
I don't care about your validation needed
For previous acts of glory
Don't be a hunter
The Never End is my story
Never ending pain , the never ending grief
It's not a simple button, I grit my teeth

My anger protrudes for the lack of understanding
Why doesn't my upset foresee it's landing
Why don't you hear, are you bored now
Is this more of a grievance for you, somehow
Okay then. I see. I get that it's me and me
I don't need you, I don't need them
I need the force of my nearest
Feeling like 10000 men

I, we, you, me,
let's go and conquer what we're meant to be

The middle

I want to do so much, so little
My mind is caught up in the middle
What anxiety drives this consistent fray
Depression matches, with such heavy days

On the outside looking in, you shan't see my pain
From the inside - I'm trying to escape from self disdain
Is it two sides of a complex coin?
Or something more where the self must join?

Even so, the physical shows
Yet the inner is red through highs and lows
Like a million bugs crawling around my thighs
I try to stay above, breathing through a million tries

You can't relax, there's no time
If it's me, the stillness, you're looking to find
You'll have to try much harder than that
Should I just hide away? Leave it at that?

No certainly not, there's more to me
Come what may, i shall be free
Where the answer lays simply in never giving up
By defining what matters, what works, and what's up?

I know the battle will hit its lows, via ebbs
Sometimes unpredictable much like a spider's web
Hello ups, hello downs what are we today?
The tingle remains, in the legs, feeling stray

I shall stay aware, I shall continue to grow
Whatever it takes to stay in the know
This nonsensical madness, like the cat and the fiddle
Is likened to me, stuck here, in the middle

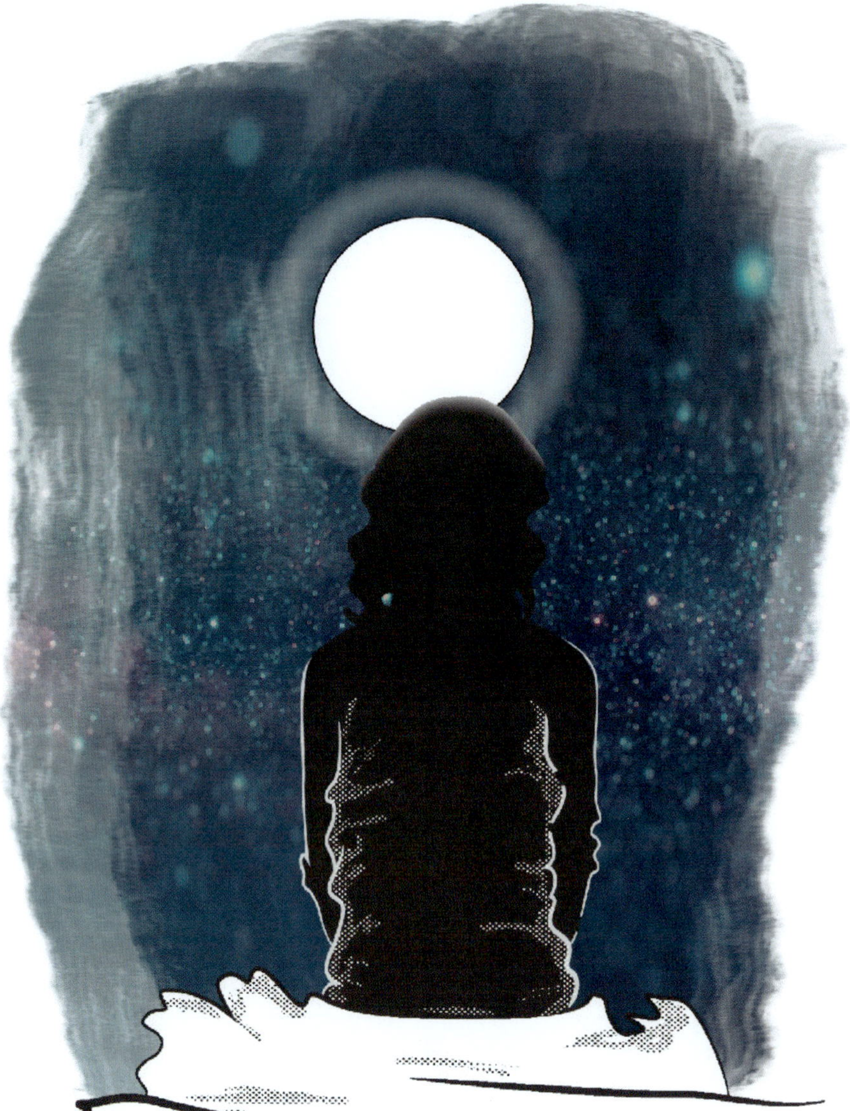

Late night

Late night memories, late night thoughts
Questioning everything that we've been taught
We're adults now do we have to be sure?
No one knows what's through the next door

What is tomorrow but tonight ongoing
Is tomorrow a secret really worth knowing?
Be present they say Be present, be now
I pray everyday that I'll soon learn how

This concept of time where nothing quite stops
Is additional anxiety for a brain that could pop
Imagine rest, imagine peace, as I nestle into desperate comfort under fleece
Should I lie, or should I wake? Should I close my eyes for sanity's sake?

The turns the tumbles, the cortex fumbles
Whilst my inner soul stays desperate for slumber
Another day done, was it good? Or bad?
Let me set eyes on the achievements I've had

Yet pressure of inner doubts stay and fight
Who needs anything when all is needed is goodnight
Accept, she says, accept your day
It does not matter, whether success or fray

Allow your peace Your inner soul to be calm
Let his hand help, and rest in your palm
The to and the fro, oh how the mind it does go
All she begs for is the steady, and slow

Today is now and tonight is here
Understand your worries, your late-night fears

For they will strengthen you, your soul so deep
You're okay, sweet girl
Now let's get that sleep

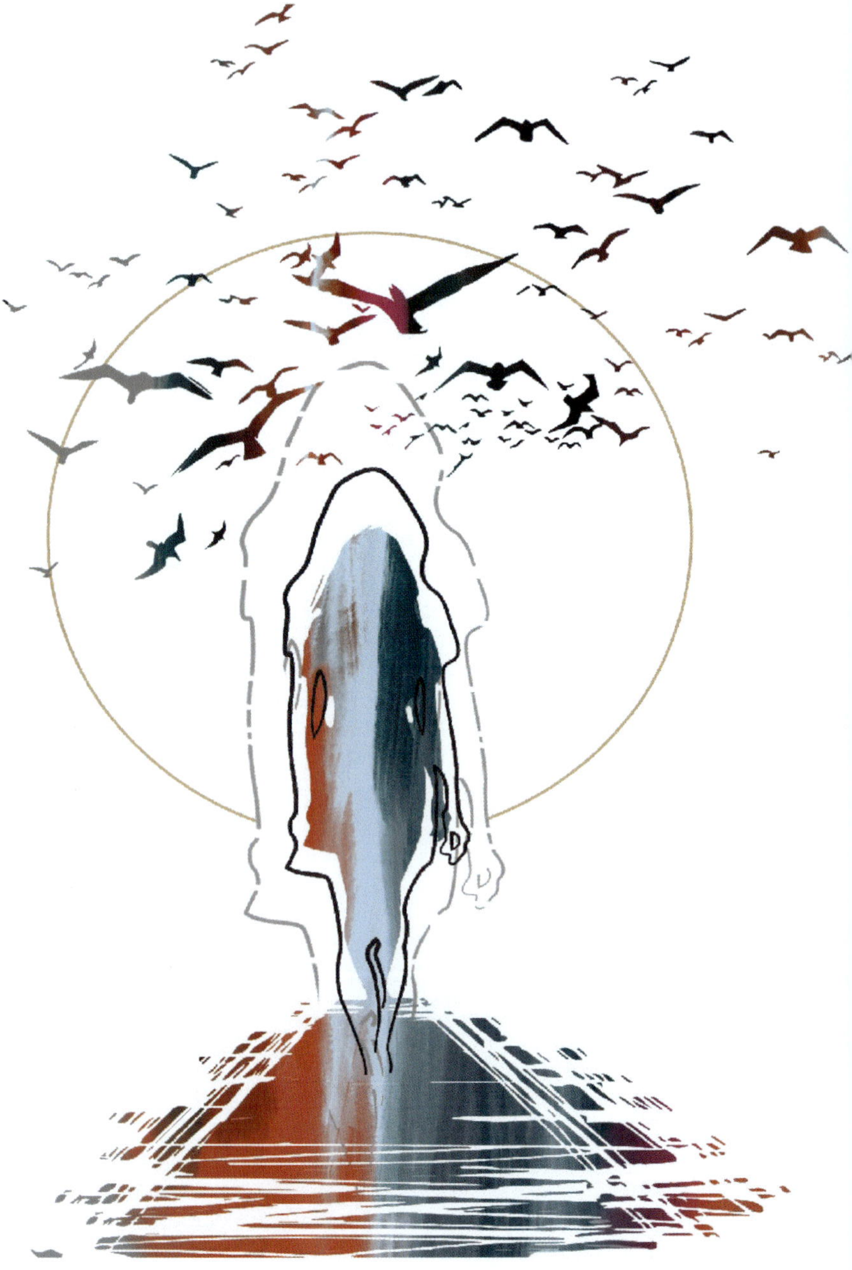

I can explain

I'm sorry the road has invited you
I'm sorry you're here to see things through
They aren't your demons to fight right now
But you stick with me, everyday, somehow

I'm not always easy, I'm not always nice
And it seems our love has paid a price
But what I'd give for a moment with you
Has seen me through the darkest hours it's true

No one is perfect, we all have our faults
And my acceptance of love is stuck in a vault
The lock is trauma and the code is pain
But I promise you I'm fighting to be open again

I'd like to say thank you for all that you do
And I need you to know how much I love you
I know I don't show you, but I don't know how
Just know that it's there, forever and now

If you could see what's below the surface
How much you give me life and purpose
You'd know that this will all be worth it
Accept the highs; accept the lows

I'm here for you, in the sun and in snow

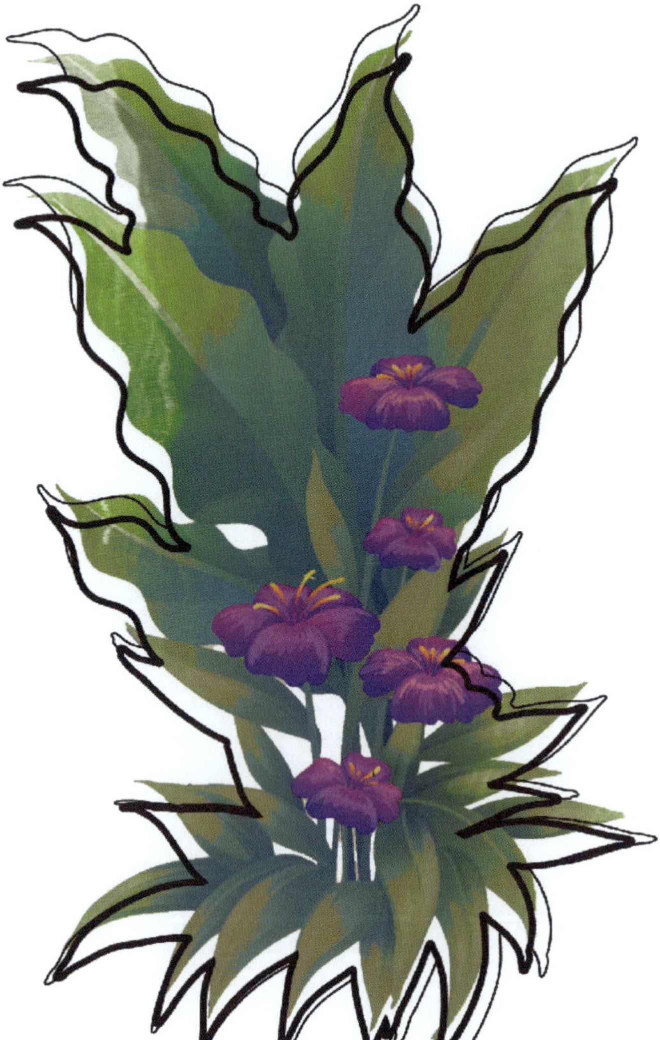

Imagine

Imagine not knowing

How much you're truly growing

Young soul

Keep going

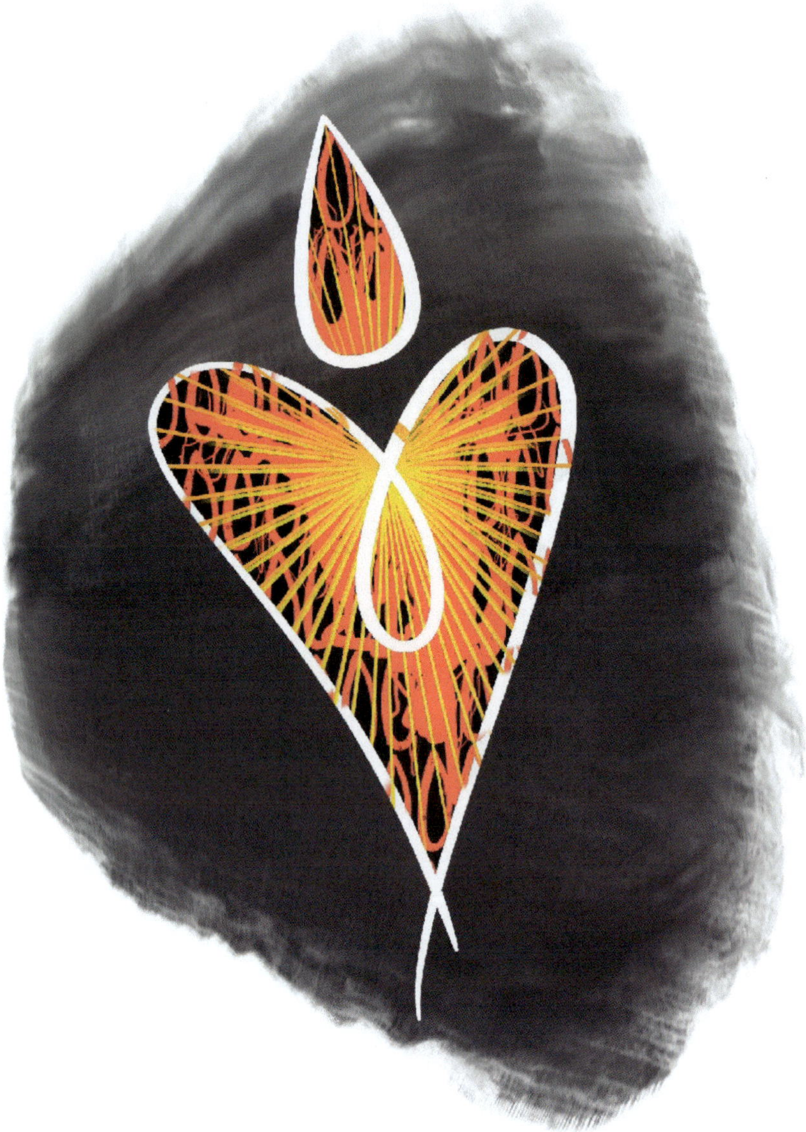

Candle

When darkness draws upon your heart
The candle has been there from the start

When all seems lost and no hope appears
The candle burns as it has done for years

When they call you broken, when you feel ashamed
The candle flickers through an abundance of pain

When you hurt so much, you start to cry
The candle stands tall knowing strength is nigh

But what is the candle?
I hear you say

The candle is your inner fire
Your reason for a better today

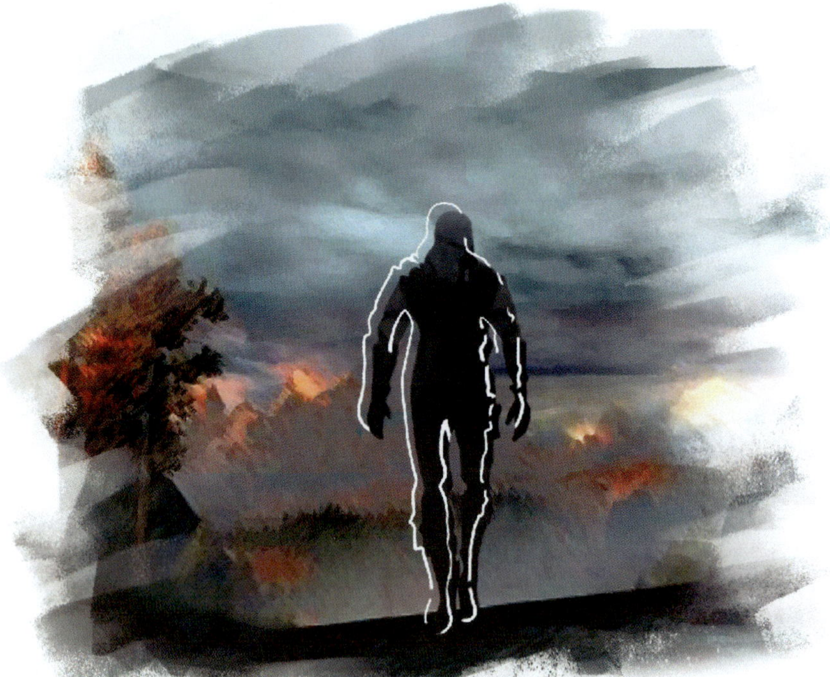

The War

The war is far from over
All is lost but one

The final battle commences
One walk towards the sun

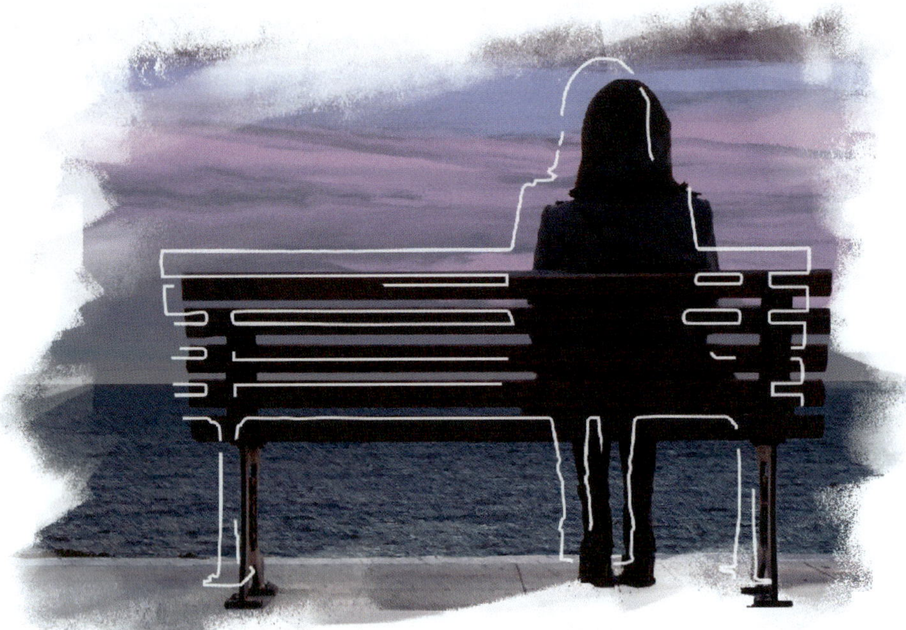

If you will not change

If you will not change
Then let me be to heal
Your actions and words
No longer provide a reaction
But a place in which to seal

If you will not change
Please leave me on my own
I'm making my own decisions now
My higher self is known
If you will not change
Accept where I am now
This higher state of understanding
A being that you must allow

If you will not change
This relationship cannot be
You see I'm healing here and working hard
Accept this brand new me

If you will not change
I refuse to be brought down
Look at what I'm achieving
Instead of deceiving
Know this peaceful town

If you will not change, if you refuse to grow
You no longer belong in my existence
In this instance I'm done with the show

If you will not change, I shall leave this ship here
I'll go my own path, avoiding the wrath to a life
That's far more sincere

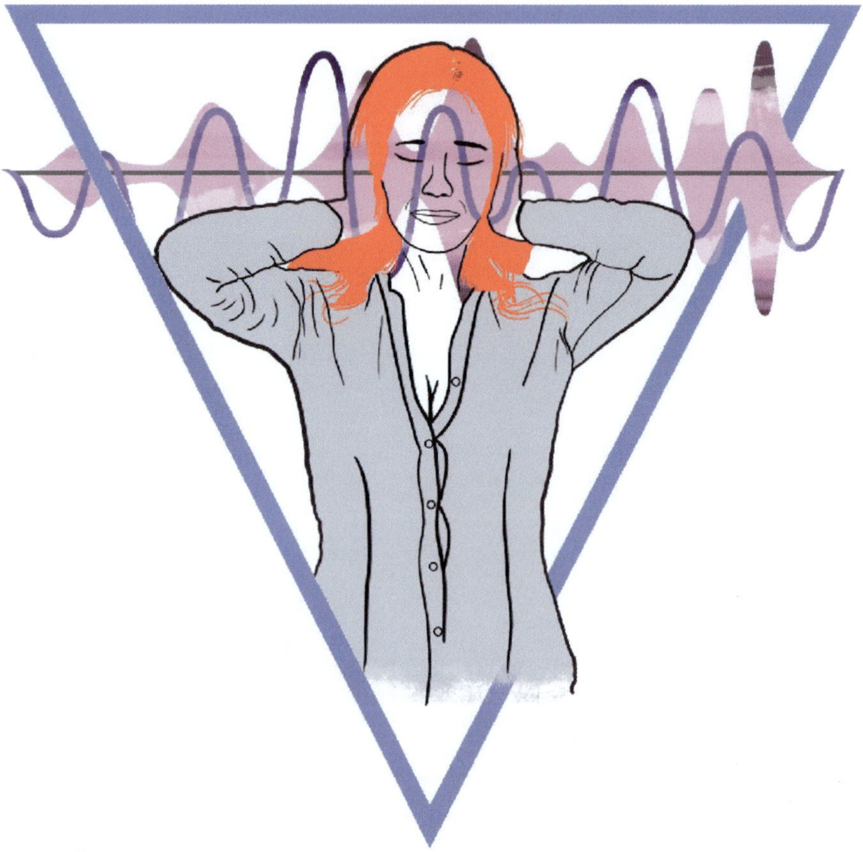

What they don't know

It's easy to ponder
To comment on one's life
To pass judgement, make comment
On another's alleged strife

One story one narrative
Is all that you hear
But for a moment, for a second
Could I make something clear?

What you don't know
Is the pain that I've felt
The courage, the guilt
The cards I've been dealt

Yes I've done wrong
Of course I've hurt so many
But what I lack in mistakes
My love offers a plenty

It's easy to judge someone
For their misdemeanours and fails
But does one look at growth?
Comment on when life prevails?

Before you seek judgment
Before you name their fall
Did you think life may be complex
Not a one word story to all

EVERY THING IS NOT FINE

Denial

Denial in others is easy to see

But I don't pick up on it when it lies within me

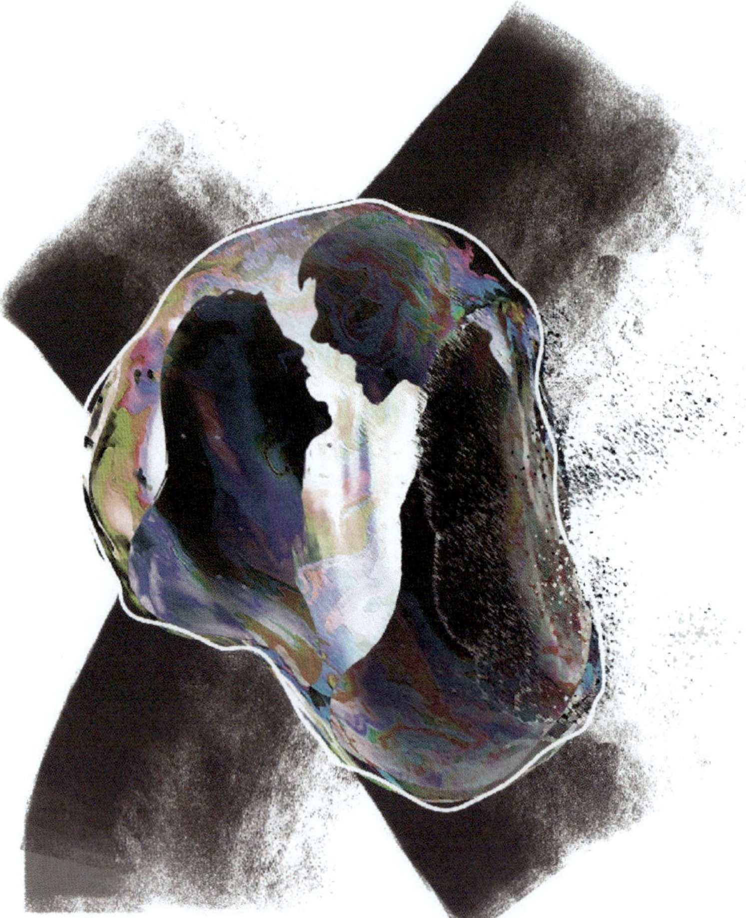

Don't judge

Please don't judge from the outside in,
This patience isn't for show; it's wearing thin

What do I do to make you see
That the inner turmoil fights that outer me

Don't take this depiction at face value
Regardless of the absolutes that you may come to

To be hyper vigilant is enough in itself
So, please know my acting lies not on the shelf
I laugh, I joke, I bring peace to others
But hear me now, my sisters and brothers

Know that I'm fighting day by day
And in fact, underneath I'm really not okay

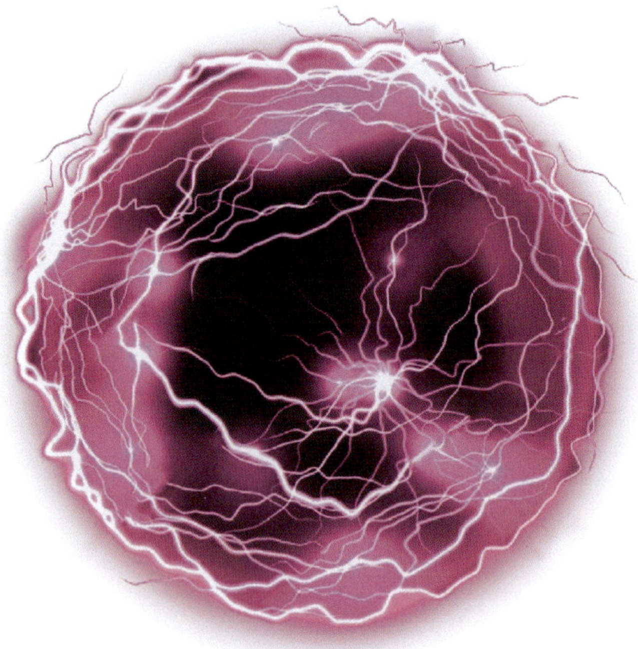

Others

Acceptance of the lack of change in others, is tough
What do we need to do, to show that we are enough?

We don't, it's simple
You are you; they are them It's beautiful
Stay on your path, "Esther Hicks" your life
No energy on others is needed at this time

The inner self, with presence, takes work
But the feeling of the now is an unbelievable quirk
Simply watch, observe, whilst others give grief
You can advise, that's it, they are yet to shed the autumn leaf

Support loved ones, yet set to remember that
Emotions and thoughts are not you, but a detrimental lender
You are above your emotions, as are others
They may not know it, but don't hide under covers

Stay bold, stay present
All we have is now
My child you will discover how not to let them in, relax your brow

I love you
Here we are
The now, this star
They are them, you are you
With this knowledge?
You'll go far

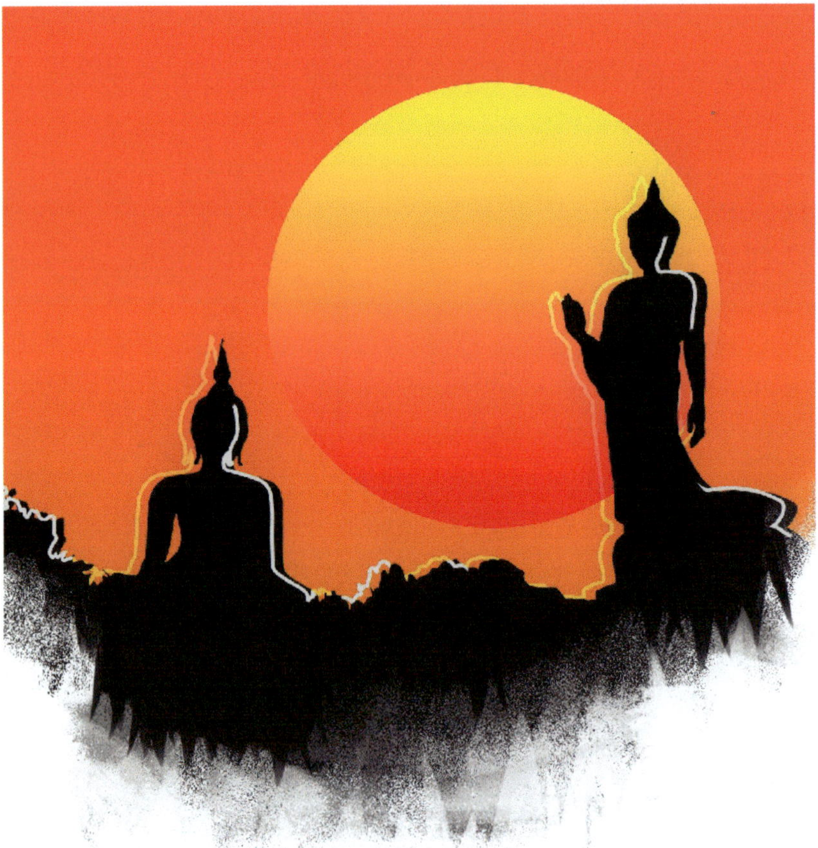

Reliance

We rely on a host of addictions
To reflect unknowingly the inner pain or position

It doesn't have to be this way
The outside world is complex but you're only you today

Reliance from within is your calling
Outer addictions are the cause of stalling

Don't put the breaks on self care
Look after every bodily atom and you'll get there

Do not shame or guilt your being
Be grateful for your awareness and seeing

Your body is you
Everything you feel is what you do

Take heed with your temple child
For life you'll need it to get through

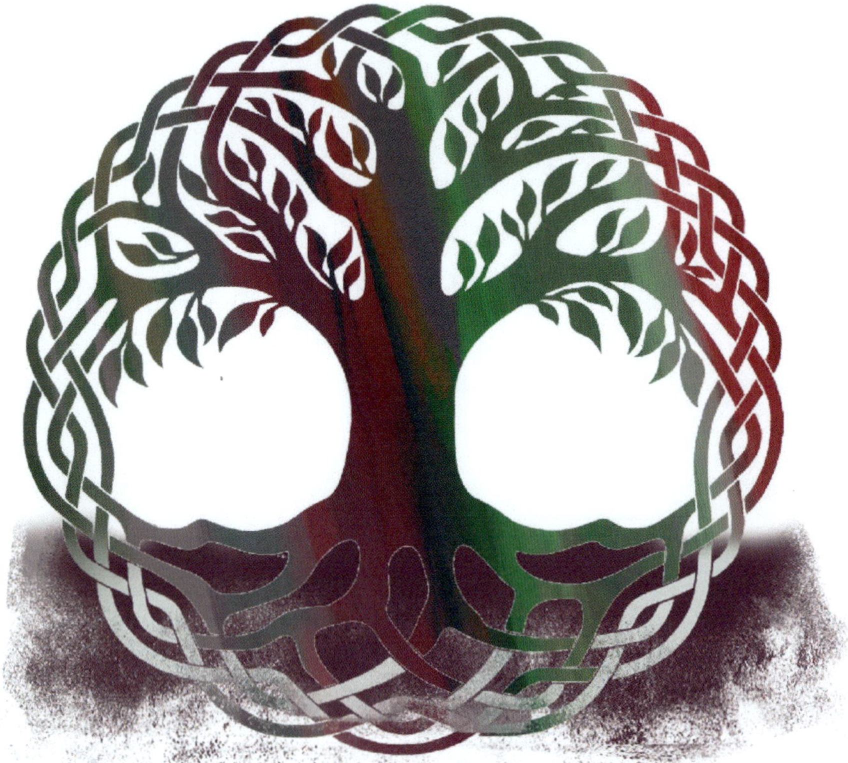

life

It's okay to feel slightly vexed, at a life so complex

Not a reason or another, there are days to expect bother

Perfection is not real, my friend

No roads will run smooth at both ends

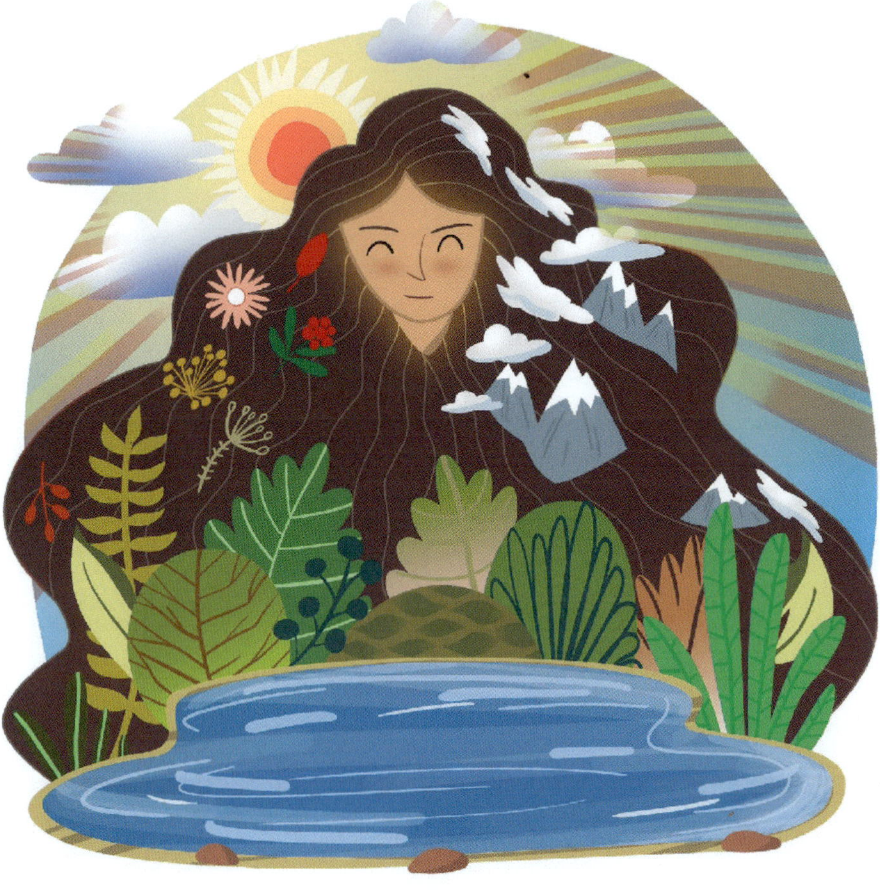

Today

It's hard to say how I'm here today
The process is wild, what can I say
What is it inside me; that keeps the fire?
There's something there; a burning desire
Is it the fight that it gave to you?
Or is it the resilience burning through?
One bad day isn't one bad week
Even if the future seems so bleak
Through thick and thin, you continue to be
Be proud of you, be proud of me
Dark is dark, and grey is grey
The colour story of my mind is an array
What is that tick? When does it start?
We get to the bottom, we find the heart
The heart, the soul, the fight to stay in life
The final thread is worth the strife
Stand up and be proud, no road is straight
I refuse to give up, I shall not be late
For the love is now, we have no choice
It's been there all along, the lion in your voice
Listen to it, what almighty power!
It'll get you to the light in the darkest hour
Well done, sweet soul, is what I have to say

It is me, it is you, who got you here today

Printed in Great Britain
by Amazon